C000029594

THE FLAME OF DIVINE LOVE

Readings from the spiritual counsels and
letters

of

Jean-Pierre de Caussade, SJ

arranged and introduced by
Robert Llewelyn

Illustrated by Irene Ogden

Darton Longman and Todd
London

First published in 1984 by
Darton, Longman and Todd Ltd
89 Lillie Road, London SW6 1UD

© 1984 The Julian Shrine

ISBN 0 232 51623 5

British Library Cataloguing in Publication Data

Caussade, Jean-Pierre de
    The flame of divine love.
    1. Mysticism
    I. Title   II. Llewelyn, Robert
    248.2′2   BV5082.2

ISBN 0–232–51623–5

All royalties earned by the sale
of this book are being given to
The Julian Shrine, c/o All Hallows
Rouen Road, Norwich

Phototypeset by
Input Typesetting Ltd, London SW19 8DR
Printed in Great Britain by
Anchor Brendon Ltd
Tiptree, Essex

Contents

Look upon yourself, then, as this green wood acted upon by divine love before it is able to enkindle it, and to consume it with its flames.

(*page 38*)

Caussade: the man and his teaching

Several years ago when discussing with the publishers the opening book of this series – *Enfolded in Love* – I happened to mention my longstanding love for the spiritual letters of Jean-Pierre de Caussade, eighteenth-century priest and scholar of the Society of Jesus. My remark was at once met with the suggestion that I should later prepare a similar book on Caussade's writings. The request, for it was scarcely less than that, has been constantly with me, even though, unexpectedly, two other books in the series have intervened.[1] Twice I have attempted the task, and twice I have shied away, feeling that the proportion of Caussade's message, to say nothing of its atmosphere, would be inexcusably lost in attempting to render sections of his finely flowing letters within the compass of a single page. However, now that the work has been completed, I have surprised myself in finding how much that is good and profitable remains, and I believe that there will be many who will be glad of the guidance of this wise and discerning spiritual director, whose writings combine the depth and ardour of St John of the Cross with the warmth and humanity of St Francis de Sales.

1   *The Dart of Longing Love* (1983) and *An Oratory of the Heart* (1984), both published by Darton, Longman and Todd, being daily readings with *The Cloud of Unknowing* and Brother Lawrence's *The Practice of the Presence of God* respectively.

It is one of the great disappointments awaiting a lover of Caussade's writings that not more is known of the man himself. Beyond the names of the places in which he worked, and the various offices which he held, we know almost nothing. In vain did I once visit (in 1971) the lovely cathedral city of Albi, knowing it had twice been the centre of his work.[1] I had hoped to learn more of one who had been my constant companion for more than thirty years and whom I now dared to count as a friend. However, to my disappointment and surprise, no one whom I met, and they included cathedral clergy and convent Sisters, had any knowledge of him, and this although he had been at one time spiritual director and at another time rector of the Jesuit seminary in that place. There certainly appears to have been no Caussade cult and it is only in the last century or so that he has become widely known. There is good historical reason for this. Caussade lived in a world which was still being shaken by the conflict between Bossuet and Fénelon over Madame Guyon and the Quietist heresy, and there can be little doubt that it was feared that the early publication of his letters might invite an examination of his own orthodoxy. In common with many writers on the deeper aspects of the spiritual life, and, indeed, probably more so than most, Caussade scattered here and there sentences and illustrations which, uprooted from their context, and examined in isolation from contrary considera-

1   See page 18.

tions to be found elsewhere, would have laid him open to the charge of sharing the heresy he is often at pains to refute. He uses several times, for example, an illustration whereby one sees oneself as a statue in the making, passive in the hands of the Master Sculptor, hammered and chiselled and chipped at the Master's will for the completion and perfection of the work. It might be said that there are strong Quietist overtones here. Yet no one in his senses would suggest that Caussade meant the example to be pressed beyond reason, and he does in fact inject into his illustrations some such phrases as 'passive acceptance', or 'obedient response' or 'patient waiting' which would be meaningless in relation to an inanimate object. It will be clear to any comprehensive reader of Caussade that there is a balance in his writing which places his orthodoxy beyond doubt.

LIFE AND WRITINGS

Although Caussade wrote one book,[1] it is in the reading of his letters – spontaneous, deeply discerning and full of warmth and vitality – that the picture of the man irresistibly presents itself. Father Joyce, SJ, writes:

> The style is the man, and from the style of the letters we get a picture of a man of delightful spontaneity, of verve and vigour, but tender, sympathetic and humorous. He is subtle but logical, humble but sure, straight, forceful and

1 The treatise on Abandonment is not here classified as a book by Caussade, it being rather an edited collection of his conferences and letters, as will be clear later.

firm yet gently persuasive and always encouraging and patient. Obviously Caussade was a man of fine character and charm and of high spiritual attainments and spiritual gifts. No wonder his treatise and letters have become one of the favourites among spiritual classics.[1]

Caussade was born in Toulouse in 1675 in which year, if we may place him in historical perspective, Fénelon would have been twenty-four, Bossuet forty-eight, and Madame Guyon twenty-seven. His two main teachers, St Francis de Sales and St John of the Cross, had been dead fifty-three and eighty-four years respectively. He entered the Jesuit novitiate when he was eighteen and at thirty was ordained to the priesthood: he died in 1751 at the age of seventy-six. The various places in which he ministered need not detain us here, but we may note that it was while he was at Nancy in 1731 – his second sojourn in that town – that he became spiritual director to some of the Visitation Sisters living there. Almost all his published letters are addressed to these convent Sisters, being written during the period 1730–42, when Caussade was between the ages of fifty-five and sixty-seven. Many letters, it is true, are not dated, but if it be correct that none were written after 1742 this may have been due to his increasing blindness, one of the few personal facts of his life which we know. Of this affliction Father Joyce writes that Caussade bore it with courageous forti-

1 Quoted from 'A Biographical Note' by James Joyce, SJ, included in *Self-Abandonment to Divine Providence* (Burns and Oates 1955).

tude and in the spirit of his own great principle of abandonment to the will of God.

Caussade's book, to which we have referred, though no doubt valuable to students as an exposition of the prayer life, is written in a dry and catechetical style and was prompted partly (one supposes) by his desire to clarify his position in relation to the Quietist heresy. Although its English translation is published under the simple title *On Prayer*, it originally bore the wearisome inscription, 'Spiritual instructions of the various states of prayer according to the doctrine of Bossuet, Bishop of Meaux', and was published anonymously as from 'a Father of the Society of Jesus'. Caussade's treatise on Abandonment to Divine Providence was not, as we have seen, originally written as a book, but owes its origin to notes of conferences and letters to the Visitation Sisters, collected and arranged by Mother Thérèse de Rosen, who was herself a recipient of many of the letters. This manuscript was circulated semi-privately after its completion in 1741. About a hundred years after Caussade's death the writings came into the hands of a deeply spiritual Jesuit priest, Paul Ramière, who edited and published them in France in 1860 under the title *L'Abandon à la providence divine*.[1]

1 English readers today know Ramière's compilation mainly through two translations, one by E. J. Strickland (Catholic Records Press, Exeter 1921) and the other by Algar Thorold (Burns and Oates 1959), though the treatise translated by Algar Thorold has also been published by Collins as a Fount paperback.

THE MEANING OF ABANDONMENT

'Abandonment to divine Providence' is probably the phrase most people associate with Caussade. What, we may ask, did he mean by it? We have already noted that the illustration of the statue in the making, passive in the hands of the Master, gives less than the complete picture. A further illustration, I suggest, may be found in considering how we learn to float. What is it that we must do? We shall at once say that we must abandon ourselves to the water, trusting it, welcoming it, giving it every opportunity to do its work. We shall know that as soon as we begin to struggle – it may be through anxiety, or doubt or fear – everything will be lost and the water will engulf us. At first sight we might think that this example is not far removed from that of the statue, for floating has all the appearance of a passive experience. It would, however, be more accurate to call it a passive *activity* for elements both active and passive are present in the process. The one who floats has throughout the operation to be making almost unseen and unperceived adjustments to correspond with the action of the ripples or waves. These movements have their counterpart in the spiritual life in the almost unrealized, imperceptible acts of faith, hope and love made in correspondence to God's action upon the soul.

The complementary nature of these two illustrations will be at once apparent, the one of the statue giving life to the agent but not to the recipient, whilst in the other the roles are reversed.

Taken together they do, I think, give a very fair picture of what Caussade means by abandonment to the divine Providence.

The above illustrations may be helpful but they are not to be seen as exhaustive. If they remain unbalanced by other thoughts they could take us perilously near to the Quietism against which we have warned. It is not so much that they are inadequate as that they might all too easily be misunderstood. For the man or woman deeply immersed in the life of the Spirit they are a safe guide, and they may, too, provide at times a valuable corrective for activists whose tendency is to be frequently one or two steps ahead of the Holy Spirit. Particularly they are well suited to the many circumstances which in their outward manifestation we may do little or nothing to change. They may be found especially applicable for most of us in situations calling for acceptance and offering, passive response as we sometimes call it. The last words are, of course, far from being synonymous with 'doing nothing'. On the contrary, such occasions call for the mobilization of all the energies of the soul for the disinfection or transfiguration of the evil encountered. It was no part of Christ's mission to come down from the cross; it was through patient offering and endurance that the victory was won.

Life, however, has many facets and if we were to call on either of our illustrations, let us say to get us out of bed on a cold morning, it is safe to speculate that most of us would be late for work. Many everyday situations such as the one we have posed – the settling down to some uncongenial piece of work, the saying of an Office when we would prefer to read the newspaper, the visiting or helping of some person in need – call for an energetic assertion of the will in the direction of some form of outward action; and although God may be seen as the prime mover in all that we do – 'Prevent [Go before] us, O Lord, in all our doings . . .', as the familiar collect has it – neither our floating nor our statue illustration will fit readily into situations such as these. It will be better here if we consider a related theme in Caussade's writing, faithfulness to the duty of the present moment. Abbot John Chapman regarded Caussade's insistence here as his special contribution to ascetic literature, expressed 'in a startling phrase, "The Sacrament of the Present Moment" '.[1]

THE SACRAMENT OF THE PRESENT MOMENT

Every moment, Caussade is at pains to remind us, has its unique and special part to play in the unfolding of God's purpose. It may be that it brings with it the impress of God's grace inviting us to some task we had neither planned nor fore-seen, and the freedom and flexibility to attend to what the Spirit reveals will be a mark of every surrendered Christian life. But, and here, too, Caussade would have us carefully attend, God's will is equally manifested and fulfilled through our faithful and prompt attention to the obligations of

1 Introduction to *On Prayer* by Abbot John Chapman, OSB, (Burns and Oates 1964), p. xix.

our state.[1] The first calls for a sensitive and gentle yielding to the pressure of God's action, the second for a generous and wholehearted commitment to the duty to be done. Abandonment to divine Providence has to be protected from the semi-quietism leading to a state of near inertia scarcely distinguishable from sloth. Caussade is alive to the dangers inherent in abandonment by those who falsely see it as an easy option to an ordered and disciplined life. It is salutary to bear in mind that his treatise and letters are directed towards Sisters who are, indeed, to learn to yield to the special and varied operations of God's grace, but this from the structured background of community life, which no less represents the manifestation of God's will. The important thing is that at whichever level the response to God is to be found, it is made from within the context of the complete surrender of the self, or, in Caussade's more familiar words, abandonment to divine Providence.

THE DIVINE PROVIDENCE

We have spoken of abandonment: what are we to say of the nature of the divine Providence to whom it is to be made? In two clear and direct sentences Caussade summarizes his teaching as follows:

Remember our two great principles: (1) That there is nothing so small or so apparently indifferent which God does not ordain or permit,

---

1 See especially Treatise, Book I, chap. I, section VIII.

even to the fall of a leaf. (2) That God is sufficiently wise, and good and powerful and merciful to turn even the most, apparently, disastrous events to the advantage and profit of those who humbly adore and accept his will in all that he permits.[1]

Everything, then, is to be seen as coming ultimately from God's hands. If we cannot see a circumstance as being directly sent, then at least we are to receive it as a part of God's permissive will. Moreover, there is nothing which may not be turned to good account if we will, by God's grace, but remain faithful and responsive in the situation which meets us.

Caussade vividly illustrates his point in the treatise by asking us to consider how the fish which leapt out of the water to devour Tobias became the food and medicine on which the next period of his life was sustained.[2] That our trials may become the strong point through which God may mediate his grace is a principle ever present and vibrant in Caussade's writings. 'Most gladly will I glory in my weakness that the power of Christ may rest upon me' is a text which takes us to the very heart of his teaching.[3]

FAITH, HOPE AND LOVE

But how is it that we are to be sustained in times of trial and distress when events press heavily upon us and darkness threatens to overwhelm us?

1 See page 8.
2 Treatise, Book II, chap. IV, section IX.
3 2 Corinthians 12:9

At such times we cannot understand God's action, nor hear his voice, and, most difficult of all, our feelings may be numbed and dry. It is faith, says Caussade, in all its bareness and nakedness which is to be our support, and some of his most eloquent writings are reserved for this theme. Faith, it has been said, is carrying on with what in our calmest moments we know to be right, even when mood and emotion are carrying out a blitz on our reason.[1] Caussade would be in full accord, and in almost ecstatic terms he writes:

> The life of faith is nothing less than the continued pursuit of God through all that disguises, disfigures, destroys and, so to speak, annihilates him . . . faithful souls endure a constant succession of trials. God hides beneath veils of darkness and illusive appearances which make His will difficult to recognize; but in spite of every obstacle these souls follow Him and love Him even to the death of the Cross.[2]

It is not, however, in the special events but in the little everyday actions that our faith will be chiefly revealed. Caussade reminds us how for the most part Mary and Joseph lived very ordinary lives. Mary does and suffers what others in her situation do and suffer. She visits her cousin Elizabeth as other relations do; she lodges in a stable in consequence of her poverty; she lives quietly with Jesus and Joseph who work for their living.[3] It all looks so very like what happens to many others.

1 C. S. Lewis.
2 Treatise, Book I, chap. II, section II.
3 Treatise, Book I, chap. 1, section II.

Wherein, then, lies the difference? It is in the faith which discerns every moment as lying within the providence of God. Faithful souls, Caussade tells us, must see God in everything for 'there is not a moment in which God does not present Himself under the cover of some pain to be endured, of some consolation to be enjoyed, or of some duty to be performed'.[1] Were we but more vigilant we would say in every happening, 'It is the Lord' and accept every circumstance as a gift from God.[2]

But, further, it was Caussade's teaching that wherever faith was present, hope and love were active too. Abandonment, he tells us, is a mixture of faith, hope and love in one single act, uniting the soul to God and his action. We have here a trinity of mystical virtues and this state of abandonment can with equal justification be designated as pure faith, pure hope or pure love. As perfect faith does not lack love, so perfect love lacks neither abandonment nor faith. In times of obscurity and darkness the soul may apprehend its state as one of faith; in times of light and blessing it will appear as love. Yet rather than talk of perfect faith or love Caussade prefers to speak of the complete abandonment of the soul to God's action, making it clear that everyone will obtain the special state God has prepared for them. Our call in Christ is simply that our good intention may be united to him so that he may guide, direct and befriend us accordingly.[3]

1 Treatise, Book I, chap. II, section I.
2 Ibid.
3 For the whole para, see Treatise, Book II, chap. I, section III.

A FURTHER IMAGE OF ABANDONMENT

Caussade supplies us with a powerful picture of abandonment under the image of a plunge.[1] We may picture to ourselves the bathers at the seaside who run headlong down the beach and with complete abandon throw themselves into the waters; and, by contrast, others (ourselves perhaps!) who test the temperature first with their toes and work slowly up and up until at last they are submerged. The twofold picture has its obvious counterpart in the spiritual life and it is clear where generous souls will stand. Caussade's own picture, however, is not of a plunge into the waters – a relatively friendly element – but into the 'deep abyss' of God's will.[2] The idea of generous and wholehearted surrender is still present but the abyss suggests cavernous depths threatening our destruction. We may believe that the image has been chosen with care for this plunge into God's will may often have about it all the appearance of loss and deprivation; and it is only the eye of faith which enables the soul to discern that in reality the plunge is not into death, but rather – through a measure of death to the superficial self – into a deeper and fuller life. It is not without significance that the picture is given in the context of one of Caussade's most passionate descriptions of the life of faith. Here in this image of the plunge into the abyss we have preserved for us the generous, wholehearted, spontaneous

1 Treatise, Book I, chap. II, section III.
2 The use of the word 'abyss' on page 30 is different from here.

and care-free nature of abandonment, and at the same time the teaching that our deepest good is often shrouded in darkness which faith alone can discern as the herald, not of death, but of a new richness of life.

THE FLAME OF DIVINE LOVE

Our book takes its title from the reading on page 38. We are to consider a piece of green wood thrown on the fire to be acted upon by the flames. It will not catch light at once but will sizzle and twist and sweat until the flame can lay hold upon it and consume it. In some such way the flame of divine love acts upon the raw material of our human nature, as yet full of imperfections and self-love. Purification and refinement and clearance of the dross there must be, and this cannot be achieved without stripping and wounding. But the time will surely come when the fire will lay hold upon the wood; even so will the divine action seize upon the soul, making it as one with the living flame.[1]

Robert Llewelyn
The Julian Shrine
c/o All Hallows
Rouen Road
Norwich

1 The illustration occurs several times in the writings of St John of the Cross and it may be that Caussade first met it there. Compare especially with the stanza beginning: 'O living flame of love/That tenderly wounds my soul/In its deepest centre . . .' St John of the Cross, *The Living Flame of Love*.

The Providential Ordering of Life

To escape the distress caused by regret for the past or fear about the future, this is the rule to follow: leave the past to the infinite mercy of God, the future to his good providence; give the present wholly to his love by being faithful to his grace.

When God in his goodness sends you some disappointment, one of those trials that used to annoy you so much, before everything thank him for it as for a great favour all the more useful for the great work of your perfection in that it completely overturns the work of the moment.

Try, in spite of interior dislike, to show a kind face to troublesome people, or to those who come to chatter about their troubles; leave at once prayer, reading, choir Office, in fact anything, to go where Providence calls you; and do what is asked of you quietly, peacefully, without hurry and without vexation.

Should you fail in any of these points, make immediately an act of interior humility – not that sort of humility full of uneasiness and irritation against which St Francis de Sales said so much, but a humility that is gentle, peaceful and sweet.

Counsel on Prayer

I have only two things to say on the subject of prayer:

Make it with absolute compliance with the will of God, no matter whether it be successful, or you are troubled with dryness, distractions, or other obstacles.

If it is easy and full of consolations, return thanks to God without dwelling on the pleasure it has caused you.

If it has not succeeded, submit to God, humbling yourself, and go away contented and in peace even if it should have failed through your own fault; redoubling your confidence and resignation to his holy will.

Persevere in this way and sooner or later God will give you grace to pray properly.

But whatever trials you may have to endure, never allow yourself to be discouraged.

On Saying the Office

As to the Office, there are three ways of saying it, equally easy and solid.

The first is to keep yourself in the presence of God and to say the Office in great recollection in union with him. Those who can say it thus need not trouble to alter their method.

The second way is to attend to the words in union with the mind of the Church, praying when she prays, sighing when she sighs, and deriving all the instruction from it; praising, adoring, thanking, according to the different meaning of the verses we are pronouncing.

The third way is to reflect humbly that you are actually united to holy souls in praising God and in desiring to share their holy dispositions. You should prostrate yourself in spirit at their feet, believing that they are much more full of fervour and piety than yourself.

These feelings are very pleasing to his divine Majesty, and we cannot be too deeply impressed with them.

The Importance of Right Intention in Saying the Office

 The fears roused about the recitation of the Office are nothing but a mere temptation, because actual attention is not necessary.

In order that prayer may have all its merit, it is sufficient to make it with virtual attention, which is nothing more than an intention to pray well formed before beginning; and this no distraction, even though voluntary, can recall.

So you can say the Office quite well while at the same time enduring continual involuntary distractions, as the trouble caused by these distractions is the best proof that the wish to pray well is heartfelt.

It is also a sign that the wish is genuine. Therefore this wish makes the prayer a good and true prayer.

Although hidden from the soul on account of the trouble occasioned by these distractions, the good intention, nevertheless, exists and is not hidden from the sight of God.

The Intention in Prayer

The fact of being incapable of sustained thought, or of producing acts in prayer, need not sadden the soul; for the best part of prayer and the essential part is the wish to make it well.

The intention is everything in God's sight, either for good or evil; now this desire it has to the extreme of anxiety – therefore it is only too keen, and has to be moderated.

The soul must be kept peaceful during prayer and end prayer in peace.

For directing the intention the soul abandoned to God need not make many acts; neither is it obliged to express them in words.

The best thing for it is to be content to feel and to know that it is acting for God in the simplicity of its heart.

This is making good interior acts; they are made simply by the impulsion of the heart without any outward expression, almost without thinking.

The chief principle of the spiritual life is to do everything, interior as well as exterior, peacefully, gently, sweetly, as St Francis de Sales so often recommends. God sees all our desires, even the first movements of the heart.

The Nature of Pure Love

It is true that love, even the purest, does not exclude in the soul the desire of its own salvation and perfection.

But it is equally incontestable that the nearer the soul approaches the perfect purity of divine love, the more its thoughts and reflections are turned away from itself and fixed on the infinite goodness of God.

This divine goodness does not compel us to repudiate the happiness it destines for us, but it has every right, doubtless, to be loved for itself alone without any reflection on our own interests.

This love, which includes the love of ourselves but is independent of it, is what theologians call pure love; and all agree in recognizing that the soul is so much the more perfect according to the measure in which it habitually acts under the influence of this love, and the extent to which it divests itself of all self-seeking, at any rate unless its own interests are subordinated to the interests of God.

Therefore total renunciation without reserve or limit has no thoughts of self-interest – it thinks but of God, of his good pleasure, of his wishes, of his glory.

It Is Necessary to Help Ourselves

How can we doubt that God understands our requirements better than we do ourselves, and that his arrangements are most advantageous to us although we do not comprehend them? But perhaps you ask that if it is sufficient for us passively to submit to being led, then what about the proverb 'God helps those who help themselves'?

I did not say that you were to do nothing – without doubt it is necessary to help ourselves; to wait with folded arms for everything to drop from heaven is according to natural inclination, but would be an absurd and culpable quietism applied to supernatural grace. Therefore while co-operating with God and leaning on him, you must never leave off working yourself.

When, in all our actions, we look upon ourselves as instruments in the hands of God to work out his hallowed designs, we shall act quietly, without anxiety, without hurry, without uneasiness about the future, without troubling about the past, giving ourselves up to the fatherly providence of God and relying more on him than on all possible human means.

In this way we shall always be at peace, and God will infallibly turn everything to our good, whether temporal or eternal.

God's Providence Is Over All

Remember our great principles:

That there is nothing so small or so apparently indifferent which God does not ordain or permit, even to the fall of a leaf.

That God is sufficiently wise, and good and powerful and merciful to turn even the most, apparently, disastrous events to the advantage and profit of those who humbly adore and accept his will in all that he permits.

I am aware that my direction is considered rather too simple, but what does this matter? This holy simplicity hated by the world is to me so delightful that I never dream of correcting it.

Let us be sure that God arranges all for the best. Our fears, our activities, our urgencies make us imagine inconveniences where in reality they do not exist.

Our misfortunes and sufferings often result from the accomplishment of our own desires.

Let us leave all to God and then all will go well. Abandon to him everything in general: that is the best way, indeed the only way of providing infallibly and surely for all our real interests.

God's Action in the Depths of the Soul

The best way of dealing with idle thoughts is not to combat them and still less to be anxious and troubled about them, but just to let them drop like a stone into the sea. Gradually the habit of acting thus will become easy.

The second way to think only of God is to forget everything else, and one arrives at this state by dint of dropping all idle thoughts, so that it often happens that for some time one may pass whole days without, apparently, thinking of anything, as though one had become quite stupid.

It often happens that God even places certain souls in this state, which is called the emptiness of the spirit and of the understanding, or the state of nothingness.

The annihilation of one's own spirit wonderfully prepares the soul for the reception of that of Jesus Christ.

This is the mystical death to the working of one's own activity, and renders the soul capable of undergoing the divine operation.

The Purgation of the Will

 This great emptiness of spirit of which I have spoken frequently produces another void even more painful – that of the will.

One then has, seemingly, no feeling, either for the things of this world, or even for God, being equally callous to all.

It is often God himself who effects this second void in the souls of certain people.

One must not, then, try to get rid of this state, since it is a preparation for the reception of God's most precious operations, and is the second mystical death intended to precede a happy resurrection to a new life.

This twofold void must therefore be valued and retained. It is a double annihilation very difficult for pride and self-love to endure, and must be borne with the holy joy of an interior spirit.

All Consists in Loving Well

Endeavour to become humble and simple as a little child for the love of our Lord, in imitation of him, and in a spirit of peace and recollection. If God finds this humility in us he will prosper his work in us himself.

Persevere in being faithful to grace for the greater glory of God and for the pure love of him. All consists in loving well, and with all your heart and in all your employments, this God of all goodness.

When God grants us attractions and sensible devotion let us profit by them to attach ourselves more firmly to him above all his gifts.

But in times of dryness let us go on always in the same way, reminding ourselves of our poverty and also thinking that, perhaps, God wishes to prove our love for him by these salutary trials.

Let us be really humble, occupied in correcting our own faults, without reflecting on those of others.

Let us see Jesus Christ in all our neighbours, and then we shall have no difficulty in excusing them as well as helping them. Besides, we must bear with ourselves also out of charity.

The Hiddenness of the Holy Spirit's Work

You have only to go on in the same way; but you explain yourself in a manner that might be misunderstood by those who have no experience of your state of prayer.

You say that you do nothing; yet you must all the time be at work, otherwise your state would be one of mere laziness.

But your soul acts so quietly that you do not perceive your own interior acts of assent and adhesion to the impressions of the Holy Spirit.

The stronger these impressions are, the less is it necessary to act; you must only follow your attraction and allow yourself to be led quite calmly, as you so well express it.

Your way of acting in times of trouble and distress gives me great pleasure. To be submissive, to abandon yourself entirely without reserve, to be content with being discontented for as long as God wills or permits, will make you advance more in one day than you would in a hundred days spent in sweetness and consolation.

Your total abandonment to God, practised in a spirit of confidence, and of union with Jesus Christ doing always the will of his Father, is, of all practices, the most divine.

The Test of Solid Virtue

When you are exposed to all sorts of criticism and unjust accusations, go on in your own way without making any change in your conduct.

This is truly to live by faith alone with God in the midst of the bustle and confusion of creatures.

In such a condition exterior things can never penetrate to the interior, and neither flattery nor contempt can disturb the peace that you enjoy.

This is to live a truly interior life. As long as this state of independence has not been acquired, virtues that have a most attractive appearance are not really solid, but very superficial, and liable to be overthrown by the faintest breath of inconsistency or contradiction.

Be well on your guard against all illusions which aim at making you follow your own ideas and prefer yourself to others. The spirit of self-sufficiency and criticism of one's neighbour seems to many persons a mere trifle; but it is much opposed to religious simplicity, and it hinders many souls from attempting an interior life. It is not possible, in fact, to begin this life without the help of the Holy Spirit, who only communicates himself to the humble, the simple, and those who are little in their own eyes.

The Strength of Peace to the Soul

The great principle of the interior life is the peace of the soul, and it must be preserved with such care that the moment it is attacked all else must be put aside and every effort made to try and regain this holy peace.

Peace and tranquillity of mind alone give great strength to the soul to enable it to do all that God wishes, while anxiety and uneasiness make the soul feeble and languid, and as though sick.

Then one feels neither taste for, nor attraction to virtue, but, on the contrary, disgust and discouragement of which the devil does not fail to take advantage. For this reason he uses all his cunning to deprive us of peace, and under a thousand specious pretexts, at one time about self-examination, or sorrow for sin, at another about the way we continually neglect grace, or that by our own fault we make no progress; that God will, at last, forsake us.

This is why masters of the spiritual life lay down this great principle to distinguish the true inspirations of God from those that emanate from the devil; that the former are always sweet and peaceful, inducing to confidence and humility, while the latter are intense, restless and violent, leading to discouragement and mistrust, or else to presumption and self-will.

The Path of Pure Faith

Profit by your experiences and never forsake the plain path of pure faith which God has made you enter upon for any reason whatever.

Do not forget that in this path the operations of God are almost imperceptible. The work of grace is accomplished in the innermost recess of the spirit, that which is the furthest from the senses and from all which can be felt.

To confirm you in this way you must remember, first, that this is what Jesus Christ meant when he said that we must worship the Father in spirit and in truth.

Second, that what is evident to the senses is only, so to say, a mark of grace.

And third, that the more simple, deep and imperceptible are the workings of God, the more spiritual, solid, pure and perfect they are.

That spirit of peace in yourself and in others is one of the greatest gifts of God. Follow this spirit and all that it inspires; it will work wonders in yourself and in your neighbour.

15

Advice to a Woman in the World

 This is what you should do during the time you spend in the country. If you faithfully follow my counsels they will sanctify this time of rest and make it bear fruit.

Approach the sacraments as often as you are allowed to do so.

Offer to God each morning the recreations of the day and with them the different pains, both exterior and interior, with which he is pleased in his goodness to season them, and say from time to time: 'Blessed be God in all things and for all things; Lord, may your holy will be done.'

In the course of the day occupy yourself about things that are necessary, and that obedience requires of you, and which divine Providence has marked out for you.

Be careful to drop vain and useless thoughts directly you are conscious of them, but quietly, without effort or violence.

Above everything drop all anxious thoughts, abandoning to divine Providence all that might become a subject of preoccupation for you.

Further Advice to the Same

As you are less busy than others, employ more of your time in reading good books, and in order to make this more efficacious, set about it in this way:

Begin by placing yourself in the presence of God and by begging his help.

Read quietly, slowly, word for word, to enter into the subject more with the heart than with the mind.

At the end of each paragraph that contains a complete meaning, stop for the time it would take you to recite an 'Our Father', or even a little longer, to assimilate what you have read, or to rest and remain peacefully before God.

Should this peace and rest last for a longer time, it will be all the better; but when you feel that your mind wanders, resume your reading, and continue thus, frequently renewing these same pauses.

Nothing need prevent you from continuing the same method, if you find it useful to your soul, during the time you have fixed for meditation.

A Biographical Note

Here I am again at Albi in a very agreeable climate, and among sociable people in whom the only fault I find is that of being too kind to me who always prefer solitude. The frequent invitations I receive are, to me, a veritable cross, and God will without doubt send me many others to temper the pleasure I feel in finding myself for the fourth time in a country that I have always loved so much.

Blessed be God for all. He sows crosses everywhere! But I have already made a sacrifice of all, have accepted and offered in advance all the afflictions he is pleased to send me.

This intention made beforehand renders trials much easier to bear when they come, and makes them seem much lighter than imagination depicted them.

Although I am always in perfect health I feel that the years, so rapidly passing, will soon bring me to that eternal goal to which we are all hastening. One of my friends said the other day that in getting old it seemed to him that time passed with increasing rapidity, and that weeks seemed to him as short as days used to be, months like weeks, and years like months. As for that, what do a few years more or less signify to us who have to live and continue as long as God himself?

Lord, Have Pity on Me

Remember the words of St Francis de Sales: 'One cannot put on perfection as one puts on a dress.' The secret you ask for I give you freely:

All that is good in you comes from God, all that is bad, spoilt and corrupt, comes from yourself.

Therefore put on one side the nothingness, the sin, the evil inclinations and habits, a whole heap of miseries and weaknesses, as your share, and it belongs to you in truth.

All that remains: the body with all its senses, the soul with its faculties, and the small amount of good performed, this is God's and belongs to him so absolutely that you could not appropriate any part by the least act of complacency without committing a theft and robbery from God.

That which you so often repeat interiorly, 'Lord, you can do all things, have pity on me', is a good and most simple act; nothing more is required to gain his all-powerful aid.

Keep constant to these practices and interior dispositions; God will do the rest without your perceiving it.

Today I Am Going to Begin

Your discouragement is a sign of a want of purity of intention and is a very dangerous temptation, because you must only desire to improve to please God, and not to please yourself.

You must, therefore, be always satisfied with whatever God wills or permits since his will alone should be the rule, and the exact limit of your desires, however holy they may be.

Besides, you must never get it into your head that you have arrived at a certain state, or you will become self-satisfied, which would be a grievous misfortune. The most certain sign of our progress is the conviction of our misery.

We shall, therefore, be all the more rich the more we think ourselves poor, and the more we humble ourselves, distrust ourselves, and are more disposed to place all our confidence in God alone.

This is just what God has begun to give you; let there be neither anxiety nor discouragement.

Each day you must say to yourself: 'Today I am going to begin.'

The Storm Must be Allowed to Pass

We ought to consider what we have been, what we are, and what we should become if God removed his hand from us.

God allows temptations or even falls that throw souls into the deepest confusion to cure them of their inflation of the mind and heart.

When God makes use of this bitter but salutary remedy, we must be on our guard to prevent our hearts rebelling against it, but submit humbly, without vexation and without voluntary agitation.

We ought not to imagine that by dint of reflections we shall be able to lessen our troubles, but should remain as if motionless in the mercy of the bosom of God, and let the storm pass without struggling against it, and without interior disturbance which would aggravate the evil instead of lessening it. We must pray for patience with ourselves and others, and for an entire resignation.

Instead of becoming strongminded we must become like children by a great simplicity, candour, ingenuousness, and openness of heart towards those who have the task of guiding us.

Remedies in Sickness of Soul

If you really have a good will, if you are seriously and earnestly resolved to belong to God, you ought to make every effort to maintain yourself in peace in order not to give the lie to the message of the angels: 'Peace to men of good will.'

The greatest evil in your soul at present is that of anxiety, uneasiness and interior agitation. This malady is, thank God, not incurable, but as long as it remains unhealed it cannot but be even more dangerous than painful to you.

Interior disturbance renders the soul incapable of listening to and following the voice of the divine Spirit, of receiving the sweet and delightful impressions of his grace, and of applying itself to devotional exercises and to exterior duties.

It is the same with such sick and afflicted souls as with bodies enfeebled by fever, which cannot accomplish any serious task until delivered from their malady.

The health of the body can only be restored by three means: obedience to the physician, rest, and good food. These are, likewise, the three means of restoring peace and health to a soul that is agitated, sick, and almost in agony.

The First Remedy

The first condition for its cure is obedience. Before all things, therefore, make your virtue consist in the renunciation of your own judgement, and in a humble and generous intention of believing and doing all that your director judges, before God, to be expedient.

If you are animated with this spirit of obedience you will never allow yourself voluntarily to entertain thoughts opposed to what has been enjoined you, and you will take good care not to give in to the inclination to examine and scrutinize everything.

If, however, in spite of yourself, some thoughts contrary to obedience enter your mind, you must reject them, or better still, despise them as dangerous temptations.

The second remedy for your complaint is rest, and peace for your soul. To acquire this, you must first of all desire it ardently, and pray to God earnestly for it, and then work with all your might to gain it.

If you wish to know how to set about this task, I will tell you.

The Second Remedy

Be very careful not to allow any thoughts which would bring about sadness, uneasiness or depression to remain in your mind. Let them alone, without dwelling on them; despise them and let them fall like a stone into the sea.

Resist them by fixing your mind on contrary ideas and, above all, making aspirations suitable for the occasion. But this struggle, while being energetic and generous, must also be quiet, tranquil and peaceful, because if it were to be restless, unhappy, ill-humoured and wild, the remedy would be worse than the disease.

In the second place avoid in your actions, whether exterior or interior, all eagerness, hurry and natural activity; accustom yourself, on the contrary, to speak, to walk, to pray and read quietly, slowly, without over-exerting yourself, no matter for what, not even to repulse the most frightful temptations.

You must remember that if these temptations are displeasing to you that is the best sign that you have not consented to them.

Keep yourself, therefore, in peace in the midst of these temptations as you have done in other trials.

The Third Remedy

It only remains to cure the weakness resulting from the fever which torments a soul in trouble. For that a strengthening diet is necessary – that is to say – to read good books, and to get accustomed to reading very slowly, with frequent pauses, more to try and take an interest in what you read than to make use of the intellect in reflections on it.

Then, further, never seek consolation from creatures by useless intercourse. This is an essential matter for those who are suffering interior trials. God, who sends them for our good, desires that we should bear them without going elsewhere for consolation, but to him; and he claims the right to settle the moment when such consolation should be given to us.

Next, we must apply ourselves, each according to his or her capacity and attraction to interior prayer, but without intense application or strain, keeping very quietly in the holy presence of God, addressing him occasionally by some interior act of adoration, repentance, confidence or love.

If, however, it is not possible to make such acts, we must be content with the good desire of doing so; for, whether for good or evil, desire is equivalent to an act in the sight of God.

Continuation of the Same

It is necessary to put this manner of praying into practice, not only at morning devotions, but also during the whole day in a quiet, easy, tender and affectionate manner by frequently raising the heart to God, or by an interior attention to the divine presence.

Finally, the best food for the soul consists in willing in all and for all what God wills; or, in other words, to adhere to all the designs of divine Providence in every imaginable circumstance, whether interior or exterior, health or sickness, aridity or distractions, weariness, disgusts, temptations and so on, and to accept all this very heartily.

You may say: 'Yes, my God, I will everything; I accept all, I sacrifice all to you; or at any rate I wish to do so and ask for this grace: help me and strengthen my weakness.'

In the most fearful temptations, say: 'My God, preserve me from sin, but I willingly accept as much confusion to my pride, and interior abjection and humiliation as you will, and for as long as you will; I unite my will to yours.'

The most uneasy and enfeebled soul could not fail to recover its lost peace and joy if it adopted these means for regaining them.

The Perception of Our Faults

What have you to fear in this abandonment, especially after such evident signs of the very great mercy of God towards you?

You are endeavouring to find help in yourself and your works, and to satisfy your conscience, as if your works gave your conscience greater security and stronger support than the mercy of God and the merits of Jesus Christ; and as though they could not deceive you.

I pray God to enlighten you and to give you a change of heart about this matter so essential to you.

You say that I should feel distressed and surprised if you laid bare to me all that you experience.

I answer that the keen perception of faults and imperfections is the grace suitable to this state, and it is a very precious grace. First, because this clear view of our miseries keeps us humble, and even sometimes inspires us with a wholesome horror and a holy fear of ourselves. Secondly, because this state, apparently so miserable and so desperate, gives occasion to an heroic abandonment into the hands of God.

Abandonment to be Embraced
not Feared

Those who have gauged the depths of their own nothingness can no longer retain any kind of confidence in themselves, nor trust in any way to their works in which they can discover nothing but misery, self-love and corruption.

This absolute distrust and complete disregard of self is the source from which alone flow those delightful consolations of souls wholly abandoned to God, and form their unalterable peace, holy joy and immovable confidence in God only.

Oh! if you but knew the gift of God, the value, merit, power, peace and holy assurance of salvation hidden in this state of abandonment, you would soon be delivered from all your fears and anxieties.

But you imagine you will be lost directly you think of abandoning yourself; and yet the most efficacious means of salvation is to practise this total and perfect abandonment.

I have never yet come across any who have so set themselves against making this act of abandonment to God, as you. Nevertheless, you will necessarily have to come to it, at least at the hour of death. Everyone is absolutely compelled then to abandon self to the very great mercy of God.

Faith in Christ Alone

'But', you say, 'if I had lived a holy life and performed some good works, I might think myself authorized to practise this abandonment, and to divest myself of my fears.' An illusion, my dear Sister. Such language can only have been inspired by your unhappy self-love, which desires to be able to trust entirely to itself, whereas you ought to place your confidence only in God and in the infinite merits of Jesus Christ.

You have never really thoroughly fathomed this essential point but have always stopped short to examine into your fears and doubts instead of rising above them, and throwing yourself heart and soul into the hands of God, and upon his fatherly breast.

In other words, you always want to have a distinct assurance based on yourself in order to abandon yourself better. Most certainly this is anything but an abandonment to God in complete confidence in him only, but, rather, a secret desire of being able to depend on yourself before abandoning yourself to his infinite goodness.

This is to act like a state criminal who, before abandoning himself to the clemency of the king, wishes to be assured of his pardon. Can this be called depending on God, hoping only in God? Judge for yourself.

This Last and Costly Step

I greatly insist on this matter, because experience has taught me that this is the last battle of grace for souls in your state; the last step to take in forsaking self and the one that costs the most.

But it seems to me that no one has ever offered so much resistance as you. This proceeds from a very strongly rooted self-love, from a secret great presumption and confidence in yourself that, possibly, you may never have found out; for, mark well, directly you are spoken to about this total abandonment to God, you feel a certain interior commotion as though all were lost, and as if you had been told to throw yourself, with your eyes shut, into an abyss.

It seems a trifle, yet it is very much the contrary, for the greatest assurance of salvation in this life can only be obtained in this total abandonment, and this consists, as Fénelon says, in becoming thoroughly tired of and driven to despair of oneself, and made to hope only in God.

Weigh well the force of these words which at first sight seem too strong and exaggerated.

Two Objections Answered

But are we not commanded to think of ourselves, to enter into ourselves, to watch over ourselves? Yes, certainly, when beginning to enter the service of God in order to detach ourselves from the world, to forsake exterior objects, to correct the bad habits we have contracted; but, afterwards, we must forget ourselves to think only of God, forsake ourselves to belong to God alone.

But as for you, you wish to remain always wrapped up in yourself, in your so-called spiritual interests; and God, to draw you out of this last resource of self-love, allows you to find nothing in yourself but a source of fears, doubts, uncertainty, trouble, anxiety and depression, as though this God of goodness said by this: 'Forget yourself and you will find in me only, peace, spiritual joy, calmness and an absolute assurance of salvation.'

But again you say: 'In this forgetfulness of self, far from correcting myself of my sins and imperfections, I do not even know them.' An error! An illusion! Ignorance! Never can you more clearly detect your faults than in the clear light of the presence of God.

In this way also, better than in any other, all our defects and imperfections are gradually consumed like straw in a fire.

A Most Dangerous Temptation

At the moment you are suffering from one of the most dangerous temptations that could assail any soul of good will: the temptation to discouragement. I conjure you to resist it with all your might.

Have confidence in God, and be convinced he will finish the work he has begun in you.

Your foolish fears about the future come from the devil. Think only of the present, abandon the future to Providence. It is the good use of the present that assures the future.

Apply yourself to obtaining attachment and conformity to the will of God in all things, and everywhere, even to the smallest things, for in this consists all virtue and perfection.

For the rest, God only allows our daily faults to keep us humble. If you know how to gain this fruit and to remain in peace and confidence, then you will be in a better state than if you had not committed any apparent fault, which would only have greatly flattered your self-love.

Ought we not to admire and bless the infinite goodness of God who knows how to make our very faults serve for our greater good?

We Grow into Deeper Freedom

 At the beginning of a new life one's conduct may seem constrained and uneasy because neither the person who is changed, nor others, are accustomed to an altered way of acting. In all things ease comes with practice.

How can a soul which is entirely employed in keeping recollected, in fighting against itself, in compelling itself to do violence in a hundred different ways, both interior and exterior, be expected to appear gay, free, happy, agreeable and amusing? Truly, if I saw it like this, I should have strong doubts of any interior change whatever.

However, are there not some people, you ask, who have a deep interior life, and at the same time appear very gracious outwardly? This is when a sufficiently long experience has made the exercise of interior recollection, in a sort of way, natural to them.

But when they began they were just like you, my dear Sister, and the same things that are said of you were said of them. They went their way without taking any notice of what others said, and God at last placed them in a state that is called the liberty of the children of God.

You Too Will Find This Liberty

Be assured, the liberty of God's children will one day be yours.

The day will come when your recollection will be without compulsion, constant, sweet, agreeable and good-humoured.

Then you will be able to add to the pleasure of others by reflecting exteriorly that abounding peace and joy which is caused in the soul by the pure love of God and of your neighbour.

Then you will be able to resume your light-heartedness and gaiety, for both will be reformed and spiritualized by the holy operation of grace.

In the beginning, however, it is impossible to do this without spoiling something.

Over-Eagerness a Stumbling-Block

Why is it that in spite of your attraction to give yourself entirely to God, and your pious reading, you seem to remain always at the entrance of the interior life without the power of entering? I will tell you the reason, my dear Sister, for I see it very distinctly; it is because you have misused this attraction by inordinate desires, by over-eagerness, and a natural activity, thus displeasing God, and stifling the gentle action of grace.

Also, because in your conduct there has been a secret and imperceptible presumption which has made you rely on your own industry and your own efforts. Without noticing it you have acted as if you aspired to do all the work by your own industry, and even to do more than God desired.

You who would have taken yourself to task for any worldly ambition, have, without scruple, allowed yourself to be carried away by a still more subtle ambition, and by a desire for a high position in the spiritual life. But, be comforted; thanks to the merciful sternness of God's dealings with you, so far nothing is lost; on the contrary, you have gained greatly. God punishes you for these imperfections like a good father, with tenderness; and enables you to find a remedy for the evil in the chastisement he awards you.

Be Content to Wait on God's Action

Abandonment to God is for you just now the one thing necessary. When you go to prayer you must be resigned to suffer exactly as God pleases.

When distractions, aridity, temptations and weariness overwhelm you, say: 'You are welcome, cross of my God; I embrace you with a resigned will; make me suffer until my self-love becomes crucified and dead.' Then remain in God's presence like a beast of burden weighed down by its load and almost ready to perish, but expecting succour and help from its master.

If you could but throw yourself in spirit at the foot of the cross of Jesus Christ, humbly kiss his sacred wounds, and remain there at his divine feet, steadfast and motionless, and do nothing else but wait patiently in silence and peace as a poor beggar waits for hours at a time at the gates of a great king, hoping to receive an alms!

But, before all things, do not dream of making any more efforts, either in prayer or in anything else, trying to be more recollected than God wishes you to be. Be satisfied to know that this state of dissipation displeases you, and that you have a great desire to be recollected; but only when it pleases God, and as much as it pleases him, neither more nor less.

Uneasiness, Foolish Fears and Depression

I can find no particular sin in your conduct, yet I perceive defects and imperfections which might do you great harm if you did not apply a strong remedy. These are uneasiness, foolish fears, depression, weariness, and a discouragement not quite free from deliberation, or at least not combated with sufficient energy, all of which tend to diminish interior peace.

'But what can I do to prevent them?' This: Never retain them wilfully; never parley with them, nor yet combat them with effort, nor violence, which would make them doubly hurtful. Drop them as one drops a stone into the water; think of something else, speak to God of other things, then take refuge in the interior silence of respect, submission, confidence and a total abandonment.

'But', you say, 'supposing that in these or in other matters I commit faults, how ought I to behave?' Well! then you must bear in mind the advice of St Francis de Sales: do not trouble yourself about your troubles, do not be uneasy about your uneasiness, do not be discouraged because you are discouraged, but return immediately to God without violence, even thanking him for having prevented you from falling into greater faults.

Green Wood for the Burning

When you throw a very dry piece of wood that will burn easily, on the fire, the flame seizes it at once and consumes it quietly and noiselessly.

But if you throw green wood on the fire, the flame does not affect it except for a moment, and then the heat of the fire acting on the green wet wood makes it exude moisture and emit sighing sounds, and twists and turns it in a hundred different ways with great noise, until it has been made dry enough for the flame to take hold of it.

Then the flame consumes it without effort or noise, but quietly.

This is an image of the action of divine love on souls that are still full of imperfections and the evil inclinations of self-love.

They must be purified, refined and cleared away and this cannot be achieved without trouble and suffering.

Look upon yourself, then, as this green wood acted on by divine love before it is able to enkindle it, and to consume it with its flames.

We Must Allow God to Work in His Way

As there is a sweet and delightful peace to be felt during prayer, so also there is a dry, bitter, and sometimes a suffering peace by which God operates more freely in the soul than by the former which is more subject to the inroads of self-love.

Therefore one must abandon oneself to God as in all other things, allowing him to work, because he knows best what is good for us.

Let us fear only one thing and that is to allow our self-will to lead us astray.

To avoid this danger it is only necessary to will exactly what God wills, always, at every moment and for everything.

This is the safest, the shortest, I even dare to say the only road to perfection; any other is subject to illusion, pride and self-love.

For the rest, drop gradually but quietly the lengthy reasonings which absorb your mind during prayer, and aim, rather, at affections, aspirations, desires for God and a simple repose in him.

This will not prevent you, however, from pausing a while over good thoughts, if they are simple, quiet and peaceful, and seem to come and go of their own accord.

The Fruit of Patient Endurance

I have already pointed out the fruit obtained by your soul in the great trial through which God has made you to pass. In spite of the violent temptations it raised in your soul, I have no doubt that it greatly contributed to your spiritual progress.

You learnt by it how to remain interiorly crucified, to be wearied of everything earthly, to make many painful sacrifices to God, to overcome yourself in many ways, to be patient and submissive and to abandon yourself to God.

Throw yourself into the arms of God and remain there peacefully and without care, like a little child in the arms of a good and loving mother.

Whoever knows how to make use of this practice will find in it a treasure of peace and of merit. Try to act thus at all times, and to adopt this interior spirit.

Nothing could be more calculated to pacify and to moderate impulsiveness and natural impetuosity; nothing could better prevent or soften a thousand bitter annoyances and a thousand uneasy forebodings.

Some Personal Reflections

God allows my sick relation to remain in the same state, to prove, and to convert the whole family. If they avail themselves of this opportunity, as I have every reason to believe they will, I shall bless God from the bottom of my heart for this happy occurrence which is worth more than all the fortunes in the world.

I am about to lose the best and dearest friend I had left, one whom I most esteemed and on whom I could thoroughly rely. God has willed it thus. His holy will be done! I commend him to your prayers.

Blessed be God in all, and for all, but especially in this, that he knows so well how to make everything serve for the sanctification of his elect by one another.

On this subject the holy Archbishop of Cambrai [Fénelon] has well said that God makes use of one diamond to polish another.

What a useful thought for our consolation! And one that will prevent us from ever being scandalized at the little persecutions of one another that good people are given to.

The Phantoms of the Mind

Ought you not to be able to overcome your fears and to check your tears after all the experience you have had of the way in which your mind creates phantoms when anything affects it keenly, making you indulge in idle terrors?

If it is impossible to prevent these tiresome wanderings of the imagination, at least endeavour to gain some profit by them, and to make of them matter for interior sacrifice and an occasion for the exercise of a complete abandonment to all the decrees of divine Providence whatever they may be.

I am of your opinion and have never desired, and still less, prayed for pains and contradictions. Those sent by Providence are quite enough without wishing for more, or inflicting them on oneself. We must wait and prepare ourselves for these; that is the best way to gain strength and courage to receive them. This is one of my favourite practices. I offer to God, beforehand, all the sacrifices that occur to my mind without any effort of my own. When, on the other hand, he sends us consolations, whether spiritual or temporal, we ought to accept them simply with gratitude and thanksgiving, but without clinging to them or taking too much pleasure in them, because all joy that is not in God only serves to feed our self-love.

Dependence on God Alone

Let us depend, then, on God alone, for he never changes; he knows better than we do what is necessary for us, and, like a good father, is always ready to give it.

But he has to do with children who are often so blind that they do not see for what they are asking. Even in their prayers, that to them seem so sensible and just, they deceive themselves by desiring to arrange the future which belongs to God alone.

When he takes away from us what we consider necessary, he knows how to supply its place imperceptibly, in a thousand different ways unknown to us.

This is so true that bitterness and heaviness of heart borne with patience and interior silence make the soul advance more than would the presence and instruction of the holiest and most skilful director.

I have had a hundred experiences of this and am convinced that, at present, this is your path, and the only things that God asks of you are submission, abandonment, confidence, sacrifice and silence.

Practise these virtues as well as you can without too violent efforts.

God Makes Everything to Serve His Ends

Believe me, my dear Sister, and put an end to all your fears and trust all to divine Providence who makes use of hidden but infallible means of bringing everything to serve his ends.

Whatever men may do they can only act by God's will or permission, and everything they do he makes serve for the accomplishment of his merciful designs.

He is able to attain his purposes by means apparently most contrary.

We shall experience more sensibly this fatherly protection of Providence if we abandon ourselves to him with filial confidence.

Quite recently I have had experience of this; therefore I have prayed to God with greater fervour than ever to grant me the grace never to have my own will which is always blind and often dangerous, but always that his will which is just, holy, loving and beneficent may be accomplished.

Ah! if you only knew what it is to find no peace or contentment except in accomplishing the will of God which is as good as it is powerful, you would not be able to desire anything else.

The Fear of Temptation

It is an illusion to have too great a fear of combats. Never shrink from the occasions offered you by God of avoiding the danger of committing sin by avoiding the struggle.

Blush for your cowardice, and when you find yourself contradicted or humiliated say that now is the time to prove to your God the sincerity of your love. Put your trust in his goodness and the power of his grace.

And even should it happen that you occasionally commit some fault, the harm it will do you will be very easily repaired.

This harm, besides, is almost nothing compared to the great good that will accrue to your soul either by your effort to resist, or even by the humiliation these slight defects occasion you.

And if your temptations are altogether interior; if you fear to be carried away by your thoughts and ideas, get rid of that fear also.

Do not resist these interior temptations directly; let them fall and resist them indirectly by recollection and the thought of God.

And if you are not able to get rid of them in this way, endure them patiently.

The Wiles of the Enemy

The distrust that makes you try to avoid the temptations sent you by God, will cause others more dangerous of which you have no suspicion.

Open your eyes, then, and recognize the fact that all these thoughts that discourage, trouble and weaken you, can only emanate from the devil. He wishes to deprive you of that spiritual strength of which you have need in order to overcome the repugnance that nature feels.

I implore you not to fall into this trap, and not to continue to look upon the revolt of the passions as a sign of being at a distance from God.

No, my dear daughter, it is, on the contrary, a greater grace than you can imagine. Becoming persuaded of your own feebleness and perversity, you will expect nothing from anyone but God and will learn to depend upon him entirely.

God alone ought to suffice to the soul who knows him.

The Good Fruits of Temptation

One would imagine, my good Sister, that you had never meditated on those numerous texts of Holy Scripture in which the Holy Spirit makes us understand the necessity of temptation and the good fruits derived from it by souls who do not allow themselves to become disheartened.

Do you not know that it has been compared to a furnace in which clay acquires hardness and gold is made brilliant; that it has been put before you as an object of rejoicing and a sign of the friendship of God? If you were to call to mind these consoling truths, you would not be able to give way to sadness.

I declare to you in the name of our Saviour that you have no reason to fear. If you liked, you could unite yourself to God as much or more than at the times of your greatest fervour. For this you have but one thing to do in your painful state, and this is to suffer in peace, in silence, with an unshaken patience and an entire resignation, just as you would endure a bodily ailment.

Say to yourself what you would say to a sick person. You would tell him that by giving way to impatience or by murmuring he would only aggravate the evil and make it last the longer.

Foolish Fears and Imaginations

You clearly perceive that your fears are nothing but idle imaginations. Therefore, if God does not wish you to be entirely delivered from them, you have nothing to do but to drop them like a stone into the water.

Take no more notice of them than flies that pass backwards and forwards, buzzing in your ears.

It occurs to your mind, I am aware, that you are deceiving everybody; but you know perfectly well yourself that you do not intend to deceive, and that ought to be enough for you.

If it came into your head to kill yourself or to throw yourself from a height, you would say at once: 'What folly! I know full well that I shall not do it.'

Put a stop, then, in the same way, to the follies and absurdities of the human mind and particularly of the imagination.

These thoughts are like tiresome flies; put up with them patiently. When these have gone, others will come and must be endured in the same spirit of patience and resignation.

On Falling Again and Again

The recital you have given me of your troubles, and above all of your faults and interior revolts, has inspired me with the most lively compassion.

But, as to a remedy, I really know of no other than that which I have so often pointed out to you; each time you have a fresh proof of your misery, to humble yourself, to offer all to God and to have patience.

If you fall again, do not be any the more disquieted or troubled the second time than the first, but humble yourself yet more profoundly and do not fail to offer especially to God the interior suffering and confusion caused by the revolts and faults to which your weakness has given rise.

Even if fresh occasions occur, return each time to God with an equal confidence, and endure as patiently as possible the renewed remorse of conscience and these interior trials and rebellions, and continue to act in this way.

If you always do so, endeavouring always to return to God, you must understand you will hardly lose anything; there will be much even gained in these involuntary interior rebellions from which you are suffering.

A Difficult Personal Relationship

I understand the keen pain you describe, the distressing thoughts that fill your mind, and all the heartache they cause. But here again, my dear daughter, is an excellent prayer if you know how to make use of it. How can you do so? In this way:

Often pray for the person who is the cause of your trouble. Keep perfectly silent, do not speak about it to anyone to relieve your pain.

Do not voluntarily think about it, but turn your thoughts to other subjects which are holy and useful.

Watch over your heart that you may not give way, in the very least, to bitterness, spite, complaints or voluntary rebellion.

Try to speak well of the person, cost what it may, to regard her favourably, to act about her as if nothing had happened.

I realize, however, that you will find it difficult in future to treat her with the same confidence without being a saint, which you are not yet. But at least do not fail to render her a service when an occasion arises, and to wish her all possible good.

In Times of Deep Suffering

Take courage, my dear Sister, and do not imagine that you are far from God; on the contrary, you have never been so near him.

Recall to your mind the agony of our Lord in the garden of Olives, and you will understand that bitterness of feeling and violent anguish are not incompatible with perfect submission. They are the groanings of suffering nature and signs of the hardness of the sacrifice.

To do nothing at such a time contrary to the order of God, to utter no word of complaint or of distress, is indeed perfect submission which proceeds from love, and love of the purest description. Oh! if you only knew how in these circumstances to do nothing, to say nothing, to remain in humble silence full of respect, of faith, of adoration, of submisssion, abandonment and sacrifice, you would have discovered the great secret of sanctifying all your sufferings, and even of lessening them considerably.

You must practise this and acquire the habit of it quietly, taking great care not to give way to trouble and discouragement should you fail, but at once return to complete silence with a peaceful and tranquil humility. For the rest, depend with unshaken confidence on the help of grace which will not be refused you.

Giving the Devil His Chance

Do not ever dwell on such diabolical thoughts as: I am always the same, always as little recollected, as dissipated, as impatient, as imperfect. All this afflicts the soul, overwhelms the heart and casts you into sadness, distrust and discouragement.

This is what the devil desires; by this pretended humility and regret for your faults, he is delighted to deprive you of the strength of which you have need for the purpose of avoiding them in future and of repairing the harm they have done you. Bitterness spoils everything; on the contrary gentleness and sweetness can cure everything.

Bear with yourself therefore patiently, return quietly to God, repent tranquilly, without either exterior or interior impetuosity but with great peace.

If you act thus you will gradually become calm, and this practice will cause you to make more progress in the ways of God than all your agitations could possibly effect.

When one feels a little peace and sweetness interiorly it is a pleasure to enter into oneself, and one does so willingly, constantly, without any trouble, almost without reflection.

Resting Only in God's Mercy

I have never said anything with the meaning that you impute to me, but have only written as to a poor beginner whom God is afflicting in his mercy, in order to purify her and prepare her for union with him.

The terrible ideas you have about your past disorders are at present what you are called to, and you must bear with them as long as God pleases, just as one keeps to attractions that are full of sweetness.

The time will come when the sight of these miseries which now cause you horror, will overwhelm you with joy and fill you with a delightful peace. Therefore do not desire any other condition either during life or at the hour of death.

Self-love desires to have, at the last hours, some sensible support in the recollection of good works.

Let us, however, desire no other support than that given us by pure faith in the mercy of God and in the merits of Jesus Christ.

From the moment that we wish to belong entirely to God, this support will be enough for us; all the rest is nothing but vanity.

The Loss of Hope

The loss of hope causes you more grief than any other trial. I can well understand this, for, as during your life you find yourself deprived of everything that could give you the least help, so you imagine that at the hour of your death you will be in a state of fearful destitution.

Allow me, with the help of God's grace, to set this trouble in its true light and so to cure you. What you want, my dear Sister, is to find support and comfort in yourself and in your good works. Well, this is precisely what God does not wish and what he cannot endure in souls aspiring after perfection.

What! Lean upon yourself? Count on your works? Could self-love, pride and perversity have a more miserable fruit?

It is to deliver them from this that God makes all chosen souls pass through a fearful time of poverty, misery and nothingness.

He desires to destroy in them gradually all the help and confidence they derive from themselves so that he may be their sole support, their confidence, their hope, their only resource.

The Purification of Hope

Oh! what an accursed hope it is, that without reflection you seek in yourself.

How pleased I am that God destroys, confounds and annihilates this accursed hope by means of this state of poverty and misery.

Oh, happy poverty, blessed despoilment, which formed the delight of all the saints and especially of St Francis de Sales!

Let us love it as they loved it, and when by virtue of this love all confidence and hope, all earthly and created support has been removed, we shall find neither hope nor support in anything but God, and this is the holy hope and confidence of the saints which is founded solely on the mercy of God and the merits of Jesus Christ.

But you will only attain to this hope when God shall have completely destroyed your self-confidence, root and branch.

And this cannot be effected without retaining you for some time in the utmost spiritual poverty.

Think Only on God's Mercy

'But', you will argue, 'of what use are our good works if they may not be for us some ground of confidence?'

They are useful in attaining for us the grace of a complete distrust in ourselves and of a greater confidence in God. This is all the use that the saints made of them.

What in fact are our good works? They are frequently so spoilt and corrupted by our self-love that if God judged us rigorously we should deserve chastisements for them rather than rewards.

Think no more, then, of your good works as of something to tranquillize you at the hour of death.

Do not reflect on anything but the mercy of God, the merits of Jesus Christ, the intercession of the saints and the prayers of holy souls.

Think on nothing, absolutely nothing that might give occasion to reliance on yourself, or to placing the least degree of confidence in your works.

Let it all be in God's Time

To avoid relaxation during the fulfilment of the duties you have undertaken through obedience, it is only necessary to do everything quietly, without either anxiety or eagerness, and to do them in this way you have but to do them for the love of God and to obey him.

But when self-love interferes with the wish to succeed and to be satisfied, which always accompanies it, it first introduces natural activities and excitements and their anxieties and troubles.

'Whatever these duties are,' you tell me, 'I feel sure that they prevent me from making any progress.' My dear Sister, when one loves God, one does not wish to make greater progress than God wills, and one abandons one's spiritual progress to divine Providence.

But the great misfortune is that self-love thrusts itself everywhere, meddles with everything and spoils all.

It is because of this that even our desire of advancing is food for self-love, a source of trouble and consequently an obstacle to our prayers.

Perseverance in Darkness

That which you say to others, or, rather, what God gives you to say for their consolation while you yourself are in a state of extreme dryness, does not in the least surprise me.

God acts thus, often enough, when he wishes to console others; and at the same time you keep yourself in a state of desolation and abandonment.

You then say what God inspires you to say without any feeling yourself, but with much sympathy for others. I do not see any sign of hypocrisy in this.

You can see nothing in your present state and still less since you received my last letter than you did before. All the better! I hope that your darkness will increase day by day, for, by the grace of God, I see clearly through this darkness and that ought to be enough for you.

Go on, therefore, through this dark night by the light of blind obedience.

This is a safe guide which has never led anyone astray and which conducts with more certainty and more quickly than even acts of the most perfect abandonment.

A Hurtful and Dangerous Temptation

The terror caused by your past sins is the most hurtful and dangerous of your temptations.

Therefore I command you to dismiss all these diabolical artifices, in the same way as you would drive away temptations to blasphemy, or impurity.

Think only of the present time in order to conform your thoughts to the holy will of God alone. Leave all the rest to his providence and mercy.

No! Your stupidity and want of feeling are, by no means, a punishment for some hidden sin, as the devil would like to make you imagine, to disturb the peace of your soul. They are real graces; bitter, it is true, but which have had and will continue to have very good effects.

I should have been very sorry to have had the foolish satisfaction of hearing your general confession; it would have been to allow you to be caught in the devil's trap.

What ought you to do, then, to free yourself from these fears? To obey simply and blindly him who speaks to you on the part of God who sent him; and think no more, voluntarily, about it.

Trials to be Suffered Until Relieved

 The suffering of the lower nature during these attacks would not be able to destroy your peace of mind if your submission to God were perfect. This is called having a solid and not an imaginary peace.

With regard to troublesome thoughts, foolish imaginations and other temptations, you must first, as soon as possible, let them fall like a stone into the water.

Secondly, if you cannot succeed in doing this, as frequently happens in time of trial, you must allow yourself to suffer as God pleases the maladies of the soul, just as you would those of the body; in patience, peace, submission, confidence and a total abandonment, willing only to do the will of God in union with Jesus Christ.

As long as your present trial lasts, you should first of all make your renunciation consist in accepting it with perfect submission.

Your spiritual troubles will only subside when you abandon yourself to all that God wills for you without reserve, without limit, and for ever.

God be praised for all and in all. Amen.

Sources and Index

There are seven 'books' of Caussade's letters and these are bound in a single volume, *Abandonment to Divine Providence*, translated from the French by E. J. Strickland and published by the Catholic Records Press (Exeter 1921). This volume, which is now out of print, also contains Caussade's treatise on Abandonment and his spiritual counsels. All the selections in *The Flame of Divine Love* are taken from this translation. In the index below, the numbers 1 to 60 in bold type refer to pages of this present book; the letter C stands for Counsel (C4 = Counsel 4); and from page 6 onwards the figure before the colon refers to the number of the Caussade 'book', the other figure referring to the number of the Letter. Thus **27** 3:4 means that page 27 of this book is taken from Letter 4 of Caussade's third 'book'.

Readers who possess *Self-Abandonment to Divine Providence* (which is also out of print), translated by Algar Thorold and first published by Burns and Oates in 1959, will also be able to use the index to refer to the selected letters. Caussade's books have also been published in smaller books each of two or three 'books'. The index will also avail here.

It may be noted that there has recently been renewed interest in Caussade and his writings. It is to be hoped that the research done in France will be available to the English reading public in the coming years.